"*Authentic Strengths* has been a game changer in assisting our youth in building resilience—using positive psychology tools to deal with stress. In an era of tremendous pressure and feelings of anxiousness, Park City School District has trained counselors, nurses, and health teachers in *Authentic Strengths*. The tools and training has built capacity within the staff and truly increased the confidence of both staff and students grades K-12 to leverage their character strengths to flourish!"

—**Ember Conley**, EdD, Superintendent, Park City School District

"Fatima Doman has had a profound and lasting impact on my university, me personally, and more recently, my daughter Aubrey. I only wish *True You! Authentic Strengths for Kids* had been written two decades ago so that my daughter could have grown up with the wisdom woven throughout this book!"

—**Dr. Sue Hodges Moore**, Senior Vice President for Administration and Finance, Northern Kentucky University

"This I can say with certainty—I've interviewed thousands of people over many years and few stick out in my mind like Fatima Doman. I thought then and now that she's the real deal. Fatima lives what she teaches, and she is among the world's best at what she does. I am so very grateful she is extending her expertise to kids. Native Americans have a saying that what we do resonates for seven generations and beyond—to teach peace, resilience, conflict resolution and more, we must start with the young. Her work and her book will resonate for generations. For that, I am deeply grateful!"

—**Donna Saul**, Host, The Greater Good Project / @GreaterGoodPro

"A remarkable contribution to the fields of positive psychology and childhood education! Applying the principles in this book will help children explore and engage their character strengths. The illustrations are captivating and the writing is inspiring. I wish all my children had this book growing up!"

—**David M. R. Covey**, bestselling co-author of *Trap Tales,* Co-CEO of SMCOV

"The best gift we can give to our children is awareness of the strengths that enable them to thrive. This book provides that awareness through beautifully illustrated pictures, as well as inspiring and memorable rhymes. *True You! Authentic Strengths for Kids* leverages the science of positive psychology to help kids discover their character strengths. The teaching helps for educators and tips for parents found in this book are also a big bonus!"

—**Dr. Sandra Scheinbaum**, CEO, Functional Medicine Coaching Academy, author of *Functional Medicine Coaching*

"My greatest hope for children is they develop a love for learning. That love comes through applying their character strengths— their unique gifts—to each learning opportunity. This book will help students recognize their strengths and guide teachers to reinforce the benefits to self and others that come with each child's strengths!"

—**Dr. Joyce Sibbett**, President, Dancing Moose Montessori School

"*True You! Authentic Strengths for Kids* is much needed for our children and families at risk. We want to influence children to become solution-focused. The best way to begin is to help children know themselves and build on their own character strengths. Thank you, Fatima Doman, you have sparked life-changing positive changes in the lives of our families at risk!"

—**Diane Williams**, MA, Stanislaus County CA Office of Education-Child/Family Services Division

"In my work role I see many people incarcerated who could have benefited from character education, people who didn't have access to these principles in their homes or schools. Authentic Strengths for Kids and the Authentic Strengths for Resilience programs are much needed for youth and families at risk—helping them discover their character strengths and respect the character strengths in others. These life-changing principles can build resilience to change the intergenerational cycle of hopelessness, substance abuse and incarceration."

—**Richard Bell**, M.B.A. Health Authority, Salt Lake County Adult Detention Center

"A significant contribution to the fields of education and applied positive psychology! Fatima Doman provides an accessible framework for helping children to maximize their potential. Cutting edge childhood education tools for the 21st century!"

—**Talyaa Vardar**, MA, PCC, Founding Partner, FLOW Coaching Institute, Canada

"A remarkable book that introduces kids to the rich, transformational world of character strengths. Fatima Doman's skillful creation of True You! Authentic Strengths for Kids has made character strengths accessible to children, which is no small feat! Research continues to show the profound, positive benefits that character strengths can have on our lives. I am grateful for Fatima's willingness to use her talents, experience, and knowledge to bring such a book to children throughout the world. Truly this book is a gift to us all!"

—**Tiffany Yoast**, M.Ed., Utah Valley University

"Whether parent or educator, you will find this book to be an invaluable resource in helping children focus on the inherent character strengths found within each of us. Share this inspiring book with your kids. Teaching children to recognize their strengths within beginning at such a young age is a gift to themselves and generations to come!"

—**Jacques Bazinet**, Vice President of Product and Corporate Development at InsideOut Development, Former Director in the Office of Stephen R. Covey

"Every child is born with seeds of wisdom, potential and a purpose in life. The role of the parent, educator, or coach is to teach the child the balanced use of their inherent strengths of character to fulfill their potential. Character Strengths are the only thing that will always be there with the child. This book will help parents, educators and coaches to nurture the character strengths of the child and to move the child closer to the inner coach. A brilliant book that will contribute to making the world a better place through our children!"

—**Sunil Tapse**, Founder and CEO of gr8synergy INDIA

"*True You! Authentic Strengths for Kids* is a powerful resource for all educators and parents. This beautiful book is a much needed resource guide for self-discovery. The powerful concepts will spark positive conversations and empower children globally to discover their strengths. Thank you Fatima Doman for your contribution to positive education and we look forward to this brilliant resource being available in Australia!"

—**Jane Wundersitz**, WunderTraining CEO, Positive Psychology Practitioner, Australian Master Trainer, Authentic Strengths Advantage and VIA Institute on Character

"The next step in bringing out the best in children! A book for kids that teaches them about their character strengths in a beautifully simplified way, enabling them to flourish. It brings a totally new perspective on education written by a truly great positive psychology coach. This book is for everyone who wants to help children live a positive, productive and meaningful life."

—**Edwin Boom**, CEO & Founder of MOOVS Training Company, Netherlands

"Current research on building a growth mindset in children has shown that helping children see their inherent strengths is the key to meet their full potential and to build resilience. *True You! Authentic Strengths for Kids* does this in a way that elevates both child and educator!"

—**Joseph F. Silveira**, M.Ed., Principal of Northmead Elementary

"As a professor, one of the challenges I see in the rising generation of students is that many of them are focused on their weaknesses and allow their fears to influence their decisions. *True You! Authentic Strengths for Kids* is an invitation to begin a transformational change among our children (and those of us who strive to teach them) as they learn to recognize and develop their strengths and the valuable contributions they can make NOW!"

—**Dr. Darin R. Eckton**, Assoc. Professor, Student Leadership and Success Studies, Utah Valley University

"Imagine the positive impact of classrooms and homes that teach children about their unique character strengths. Every parent and educator should read this book with the children they influence!"

—**Murat Vardar**, President, Flow Coaching Institute Turkey

"A great book to talk about character strengths with kids. Beautiful illustrations for every character strength. A must have for every parent and within every school!"

—**Roosje Boom Van Gelder**, Commercial Director Moovs, ASA Master Facilitator, Benelux

"What I love most about *True You! Authentic Strengths for Kids* is it actually teaches complex science-based tools in positive psychology that are broken down for children in a way that is fun, easy to understand and remember. Fatima Doman explains these concepts so that it offers a parent hope with greater understanding. Our students and children need solution focused examples of resiliency, perseverance, and grit and this book provides a beautifully illustrated way to reach and teach them! This will be the "go to" children's book for empowering and strengthening little leaders in your own life and teaching the developmental assets in their community!"

—**Dr. Jaynee Poulson**, CEO, The Give Back Program, Former Utah State PTA Health Commissioner

"Helping children, and their parents, recognize and understand their personal strengths at an early age will make a definite difference in developing an everlasting happiness throughout their life. Explaining and coaching authentic strengths and positive psychology to children and adults is clearly one of Fatima Doman's many strengths. My own learnings from Fatima's book have changed my approach to life balance and there is no doubt that her new book will help shape and improve the lives of many children and of their parents!"

—**Marc Noël**, Father, Grandfather, Entrepreneur

"The lessons went great! There was so much discussion, and I had students who rarely participate and share go the extra mile and really learn a lot about themselves. In one activity, they wrote 'Thank You' notes to people they wanted to show appreciation to. The expressions on the faces of the recipients were incredible. Thank you for sharing your tools with us. It really works!"

—**Jared Romero**, Educator, Park City School District

"*True You! Authentic Strengths for Kids* is like a modern-day Doctor Seuss! The simplicity of the message and wide range of strengths combine to make compelling motivational reading!"

—**Alexis Chadderdon**, President, Junior League of Lansing Michigan

TRUE YOU!
Authentic Strengths for Kids

Fatima Doman
with Kristen B. Walton
Illustrated by Whitney W. Wilding

TRUE YOU
Authentic Strengths for Kids

Published by Next Century Publishing
Austin, TX
www.NextCenturyPublishing.com

ISBN: 978-1-68102-659-6

Printed in the United States of America

TIPS FOR PARENTS and EDUCATORS

Moving from "What's Wrong" to "What's Strong"

Imagine you found a flower bud in your garden—you see the bud, but are unsure what flower will unfold from it. If you have a predetermined wish or requirement for it to be one vs. another, such as wanting an orchid to be a geranium or a tulip to be a rose, you will be disappointed when the "wrong" one unfolds. You will focus on what's wrong with it and try to make it what you want it to be, and in so doing may harm it and prevent it from reaching its potential.

What if, as parents and educators, we could learn how to appreciate a child's authentic character strengths rather than trying to mold him or her into some preconceived ideal? How would that positively impact a child's learning, achievement and overall development?

Dr. Martin Seligman, the father of positive psychology, revealed in his ground-breaking research that once people know what their best qualities are, they open up a vital pathway to engagement—at school, at work, in relationships and in life. Due to this new science, we now can help people identify the character strengths that define who they are at their best. The qualities that, when nurtured, can lead to good outcomes in every aspect of their lives. Developing an awareness of these strengths helps people to focus on "what's strong" (their strengths), instead of "what's wrong" (their weaknesses). As two decades of research and hundreds of studies have now shown, people who express their strengths tend to be happier, more resilient, less stressed and higher achievers.

Character strengths are the most important aspect of ourselves that we want recognized and understood by others. They are collectively responsible for our greatest achievements and fulfillment. Positive psychologists have identified twenty-four strengths—the basic building blocks that represent our individuality, psychologically speaking. We each possess all twenty-four in varying degrees and combinations. These strengths are universally valued around the world and scientists define them as positive traits that are beneficial to self and others. They lead us to positive emotions, relationships, and into engaging and meaningful life activities where we flourish.

In my twenty years of coaching, I have yet to encounter a more powerful tool for growth. I have witnessed dramatic positive change when people understand and use their strengths, while appreciating the strengths in others. Visit AuthenticStrengths.com to discover your unique strengths profile!

Your coach,

You're exceptional, awesome, and wonderful too!
You are full of good traits that help you be you.
Traits are called character strengths. There are 24.
You were born to do great things with them, I am sure.

Strengths grow like muscles and fill you with glee,
they help you in school, and with friendships you see.
Everyone has strengths, isn't that great?
It's time to discover yours now, let's not wait!

When you play make believe,
or you draw in a book,
or you build with some blocks you're
creative, just look.

If you **appreciate beauty** around you it means you are someone who notices beautiful scenes.

Do you feel **brave** as you try something new?
It's courage that's helping you know what to do.

When you look at the places you want to explore,
that's **curiosity** helping you want to know more.

Showing **fairness** is fun as you each take your turn.

You share, and you love, and you laugh, and you learn.

Seeing the big picture is so very wise.
It's what's called **perspective** that opens your eyes.

Being **honest** and strong puts you up to the test.
Honesty knows that the truth is the best.

If someone does something that makes you feel sad.
But then they say sorry their actions were bad.
As you show **forgiveness**, in a short while,
frowns and bad feelings will turn to a smile.

When you notice your blessings in life overflow,
it is **gratitude** filling your heart you should know.

Are you feeling **hope** as you look at your day?
You're optimistic and sure of good things on the way.

Showing **kindness** in words and kindness in deeds
to yourself and to others, that's what the world needs.

When you make people giggle you are playful and fun.
Humor warms us inside like the rays of the sun.

Strong **leadership** lifts and helps others feel good.
You inspire their best like a good leader would.

When you're **open-minded** as you look ahead
at the fork in the road and which path you will tread,
You weigh your decisions so you won't get lost.
Your judgement will help you whatever the cost.

Love is a strength to be shared it is true,

and sharing helps love to swing right back to you.

As you read, read, read, read and **love learning** new things you gain many new skills and the joy that it brings.

When you start you will finish, you're **persistent** my friend.
You climb to the top and won't quit 'til the end.

It is wise to be **prudent**.
That's how you roll.
You are careful and cautious
making safety your goal.

Spirituality brings purpose and meaning to you as you look at your life and decide what you'll do.

When you're good at a sport or at playing a note,
you act **humble** and kind, you are not one to gloat.

As you handle your actions, you know what to do.
You are under control and are **disciplined** too.

Linked together you're loyal and work at your best.
With **teamwork** you're sure to look out for the rest.

Social intelligence means you are very aware
of how to make friends and show them you care.
You understand others, how they think, how they feel.
The friendships you make will last long and be real.

When you're feeling alive you are filled with such zest.
Being happy and peppy you give life your best!

Which strengths make you happy and feel at your best?
You can use those a lot, and can strengthen the rest.
Your life is a gift to this world, you should know.
It makes the world better when strengths really show.
There's no limit to all the good things you can do.
You are one of a kind and uniquely TRUE YOU!

TEACHING HELPS

True You! Authentic Strengths For Kids

Before reading

- Talk to children about the words "character strengths" and what it means to be strong in this way. Explain to children these strengths will help them do better in school, be more resilient and get along better with others.

- Set a purpose: Ask children to think of 2 or 3 things they feel they are good at, like to do, or that bring them joy. Prepare the children to think about how specific character strengths match what they like to do as you identify the character strengths during reading.

- Introduce new vocabulary words by pointing out the unfamiliar words as you read them to the children. Clarify these new words with context clues.

During reading

- Pause occasionally and provide relatable examples of experiences that might match certain character strengths.

- Using the Authentic Strengths card deck (found at AuthenticStrengths.com), or making your own flash cards with pictures and words to represent the 24 character strengths, place cards on the board during reading of each strength so that when you are finished, all character strengths are displayed. During future projects, you can have the children refer to the cards to remind them of the 24 character strengths and examples of how they can be used.

After reading

- Have children write a story about themselves using one of their top character strengths.

- Create a matching game by finding images of children using character strengths and have children match them with the corresponding character strength.

- Have children share with a partner a character strength they noticed in themselves or another student/friend/family member, during the story.

- Have children create a painting, drawing or art project that shows the child using a character strength that makes them feel happy and full of energy.

Further discussion

- Create a new purpose: Each time the book is read, remind children that they have all 24 character strengths, some are used more and some are used less. Have the children identify the top 5 character strengths that describe them best. The 5 strengths that they identify are their "top 5 strengths" and are their favorite ones to use. This is significant in helping them begin to realize where they are strong. Help children strategize ways to build less used character strengths. Remind them that they can build any character strength any time the situation calls for it.

www.AuthenticStrengths.com

ABOUT AUTHENTIC STRENGTHS ADVANTAGE®

Our mission is helping people engage their character strengths to increase their resilience, achievement and fulfillment in all aspects of life. The Authentic Strengths Advantage® evidence based coaching, training and certification programs are a game changer. Appreciating and leveraging strengths creates a culture of mutual respect where individuals are empowered to be their best selves. Our process and tools inspire people to be authentic in all aspects of life, creating the conditions for sustainable high performance—the key to human motivation and engagement.

Visit us at AuthenticStrengths.com to take the free VIA strengths survey and discover your own, unique strengths profile. Join our learning community at info@authenticstrengths.com to share your insights using the Authentic Strengths® tools in this book, or to inquire about workshops and certifications near you.

About VIA

In 1998, Dr. Neal H. Mayerson and then President of the American Psychological Association, Dr. Martin E.P. Seligman, conceived a robust effort to explore what is best about human beings and how we can use those characteristics to build our best lives. They launched an effort of unprecedented magnitude to lay the groundwork for the new science of positive psychology. A diverse collection of scholars and practitioners took three years and more than a million dollars of funding to develop the VIA Classification of Character Strengths and Virtues and the VIA Surveys for adults and youth. The enormous response of millions of people worldwide taking the surveys has made it clear that VIA's work is resonating broadly and deeply.

ABOUT THE BOOK CONTRIBUTORS

Fatima Doman, CEO of Authentic Strengths Advantage®, Speaker and Coach is passionate about helping people to use their character strengths for greater resilience, engagement and fulfillment. In this book, she shares positive psychology tools for children, parents and educators based on her insights from over two decades of coaching high performers around the globe. Fatima's bestselling book, Authentic Strengths, has been featured by the Huffington Post, Psychology Today, and on TV and Radio. Her coaching certifications and workshops have been licensed globally.

Fatima believes that self-awareness plays a key role in reaching our potential, and that each of us can develop our strengths to realize our aspirations and overcome our challenges. Drawing on groundbreaking psychology and neuroscience research, Fatima reveals pathways to wellbeing, happiness, sustainable achievement and positive relationships. She demonstrates how engaging our strengths, while appreciating strengths in others, boosts our emotional intelligence and transforms our effectiveness in all areas of life.

Fatima holds an MA from California State University and the Advanced Executive Coaching Certification from Columbia University. She has served as Co-Founder of FranklinCovey's Global Executive Coaching Practice and on Faculty of the FranklinCovey/ Columbia Business School Executive Coach Certification Program.

Fatima's greatest joy comes from spending time with her family and friends.

**Kristen Walton brings to Authentic Strengths Advantage®
a wealth of experience having served many years volunteering in
leadership positions with multiple youth organizations fostering the
development of children and teens.** Kristen loves working with kids!
She has a passion for helping children see their worth—even from a very
young age.

Kristen's career has taken her through many aspects of design
where her creative passion is put to use, including in the writing of this book. Kristen currently
owns her own company, Inside Out Designs, and loves spending time with her family and hiking
with her dog.

**Whitney Wilding brings to her role as education consultant
at Authentic Strengths Advantage® many years of experience as a
public elementary education professional.** She received her BA in
Elementary Education from Brigham Young University.

Whitney uses her artistic talent illustrating. Energized by her life-
long love of children's books, Whitney strives to spark imagination and
wonder in the minds of her readers. She can be found most often
spending time with her husband and dog, Sadie.

Contact us at: AuthenticStrengths.com